The Biggest Animal Ever

By Allan Fowler

Consultants:

Robert L. Hillerich, Ph.D., Bowling Green
State University, Bowling Green, Ohio

Mary Nalbandian, Director of Science,
Chicago Public Schools, Chicago, Illinois

Fay Robinson, Child Development Specialist

CHILDRENS PRESS®
CHICAGO

Design by Beth Herman Design Associates

Library of Congress Cataloging-in-Publication Data

Fowler, Allan
    The biggest animal ever / by Allan Fowler.
      p. cm. –(Rookie read-about science)
    Summary: Briefly describes the physical characteristics
and behavior of whales.
    ISBN 0-516-06001-5
    1. Whales–Juvenile literature. [1. Whales.] I. Title.
  II. Series: Fowler, Allan. Rookie read-about science.
QL737.C4F68 1992
599.5–dc20   92-9410
                                     CIP
                                     AC

Do you know which
animal is the biggest
one ever?

It's an animal alive today —
the blue whale.

This animal weighs
more than the biggest
dinosaur that ever lived.

Whales are mammals, even though they look like fish.

Dogs and cats, horses and elephants — people, too — are mammals.

Like almost all mammals, baby whales are born from their mother's body, not from eggs.

A baby whale is called a calf. It feeds on milk from its mother's body.

And like all mammals,
whales breathe air.

A whale can stay
underwater a long time.

12

But it must come up to
the surface to breathe.

When you see whales
spout, they are breathing.
They blow out the old air
through a blowhole on
top of their head.

Whales are among the smartest animals.

They can hear underwater.

It is possible that they hear sounds from hundreds of miles away.

Whales whistle, grunt,
and sing to each other.

Scientists have studied
these whale "songs."

Are whales talking?
Well, they seem to
understand each other!

Dolphins and porpoises are very much like whales.

They are very friendly
and love to play.

At marine parks, you can
see dolphins leap high out
of the water.

Not too long ago, whales were hunted and killed. People wanted oil from the whales to burn in lamps.

But the hunters killed too
many whales. Some kinds
of whales were almost lost
forever.

Now there are laws to
protect whales from harm.

There are boats that take
people where they can
learn about whales without
bothering them.

The biggest animal that ever lived deserves our best care.

Words You Know

whales

blue whale

breathing

blowhole

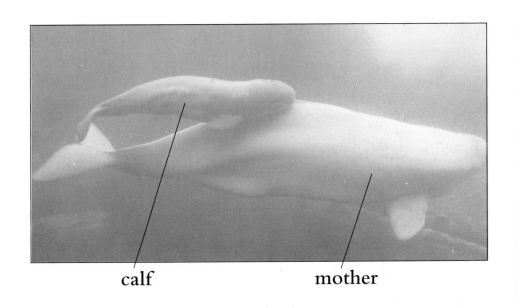

calf   mother

dolphin

mammal

31

Index

About the Author

Allan Fowler is a free-lance writer with a background in advertising. Born in New York, he lives in Chicago now and enjoys traveling.

Photo Credits

A/P Wide World Photos – ©Ed Baily, 8, 31 (top)
marine mammal images – ©Mark Conlin, 6
PhotoEdit – ©Myrleen Ferguson, 7, 31 (bottom right)
Jeff Rotman Photography – ©Bob Cranston, 11; ©Itamar Grinberg, 20
©1992 Sea World of Florida – 22, 31 (bottom left)
SuperStock International, Inc. – 24, 25
Valan – ©Richard Sears, Cover, 4-5, 12, 15, 28, 30 (3 photos); ©Kennon Cooke, 9, 21; ©Fred Bruemmer, 16; ©Jeff Foote, 19, 26, 27; ©Francis Lépine, 23
COVER: Blue Whale

1/98

1MM4